how to live with an

αlpha female

Dear Ashley & Sojin, *20/5/17*

Murray Partridge
and
Simon Marks

Lots of love,

Simon xx

How to live with an Alpha Female
Copyright © Simon Marks and Murray Partridge, 2017

First published in 2017 by Markridge

ISBN: 978-1-911195-42-9

To our AFs. Obviously.

Contents

A word from the authors

I was sitting in a café one sunny day flicking through a glossy magazine. I got to the photo-montage section that showed a double page of well-known people enjoying a 'society' party, and my wife was one of them.

This sort of thing happened quite a lot and until that point I hadn't really given it much thought. I felt it was just an aspect of her work. But on this occasion I noticed that the photograph looked slightly odd. Her arm was in a strange position and the area to her left-hand side looked a little blurred and unreal. After pondering for a while, I realised the photo looked odd because somebody had been 'airbrushed' out of the shot. Somebody who had been standing next to my wife, interlocking arms with her.

Then I realised that that person was me!

All of a sudden, and for the first time, it all became clear to me. I was married to a woman who was more important than me. More photo-worthy, more note-worthy, more interesting, more successful, more significant. I was a bit part player in the life of an Alpha Female. Indeed, I was married to an Alpha Female.

The sudden realisation explained so many things about my life that I had not, perhaps by choice, fully recognised before. It may sound ridiculous that I didn't realise she was an AF but I had been married to her for quite some time, and for the first few years she was a humble shop girl. I was the breadwinner with a reasonably snazzy job as the creative director of an ad agency. I suppose I felt I was in charge.

The shift in our relationship and her success had happened over a period of ten years and I had been so wrapped up in my own stuff that I hadn't really noticed that she had grown into another person and overtaken me in every area.

Over those years she had set up a business and become financially successful. She had become more confident and more articulate. As I had become fatter, uglier and balder she had become more alive and more beautiful. Her energy levels and her appetite for life had increased as mine had decreased. She had become well known enough for the paparazzi to snap her at premieres and parties. I had slipped from Alpha Male to Beta Male. She had grown from Beta Female to Alpha Female.

Obviously I don't want to seem ungrateful for her success in life and in fact I'm profoundly not. The 'compensations' for being outstripped by my wife have been considerable. She earns [and this bit is hard to say] almost exactly twenty times as much as me so recently I have been able to stop worrying about money [although worrying about money is so deeply ingrained that I still do].

She has access to people and places that I would never have gained without her. Her world is rich and full so I never have to deal with a disappointed and under-stimulated wife.

And because she is an AF she takes care of EVERYTHING. Everything in my life is organised, staffed, sorted, paid for, polished, filed, perfected and invisibly taken care of. Fresh toothbrushes appear every four weeks. The beds remake themselves. The holidays get booked. Thank-you notes get written. The fridge is always full. The garden is tended. The dinner gets cooked. Everything is perfect because my wife is an Alpha Female.

This small book is an attempt to lay out some of the things I've learnt from being married to an AF.

Some of the lessons, some of the gripes, some of the advantages, some of the rules of the game. A few male friends of mine are in the same position as me and some of those have contributed to this book with their thoughts and observations too.

My co-author, Simon, whose wife is also an AF of the highest order, has joined with me to collate and write up our observations and those of our friends...

I hope the book will be a useful manual for any man and any woman who find themselves in this unusual and very modern kind of relationship.

Murray Partridge

Ignorance can be bliss ... and it was until one day in 2011, when, casually at a party, I was informed that I was married to an Alpha Female.

Up until that point I think I just thought my wife was strong-willed and good at getting her own way [which of course she is]. However, as I soon came to discover, these traits are just a couple of the distinguishing features of the ever-increasing growing population of Alpha Females.

Nothing had really registered that my 'more significant' wife might be an Alpha Female. In fact, I'm not even sure I knew what they were, or acknowledged that they existed, and I certainly didn't know what characteristics I should be looking out for.

However, in the twelve months that followed, with my co-author's help, I slowly began to notice, identify and label more traits that pointed to the fact that my partner was, in all likelihood, an Alpha Female. It also began to dawn on me that there was the possibility that, unlike most men, I hadn't married my mother, I had in fact married my [Alpha] father.

Unlike Murray, I knew from the start I was married to a woman who was more important than me, more photo-worthy, more note-worthy, more interesting, more successful, and more significant. Her accomplishments are many and varied. As well as having a business, she's written books, produced films, worked with royalty, and her substantial address book of friends and contacts are an impressive and wonderful gang of movers and shakers.

I had entered this relationship on the back of a happy and successful seventeen years in the music business, and took great pride in having overseen the release of some fantastic music by some amazing artists. However, whilst I was slogging away, simply releasing the music of great artists, the woman who was to become my wife was out having dinner with them, holidaying with them, and in some instances was even godmother to their children.

I came to understand that part of having an Alpha Female for a partner is accepting that whatever you've done, your AF has probably done it bigger and better. In my case, she has also done many of the things that, as a man, I'm meant to have done, scuba-dived around the world, heli-skiing, car racing, produced films about sex, worked for Playboy magazine, etc, and so on.

Perhaps my co-author and I are the forerunners of the future husband who will have to learn how to play in the shadow of Alpha Females. The reality, of course, is not that some women are alpha and some are not. The truth is that, just like men, there is a little bit of alpha in every woman, and, as women slowly take over the reins of power, the Alpha Female is becoming more common and more noticeable. The world is changing and any man who believes he will be enjoying age-old patriarchal privileges in the coming decades is living in denial.

With this in mind, as your ambitions are outshone by your Alpha partner's achievements, there might be some wisdom in retreating to be seen but rarely heard. With the risks entailed at jumping out of the shadows of our Alpha Females, and laying them open to the world, here is a book that we hope will not only help Alphas and their partners live in harmony, but have a laugh along the way.

As you read through the book, don't confuse what sounds like a little bitterness and criticism, for what in reality, is simply love and a lot of admiration.

Alpha Females can be a tricky proposition, but if you're lucky enough to have one, rejoice – who wants a Sunday afternoon stroll in the park when you can have a seven-day-a-week roller coaster.

Simon Marks

Two careers

As the husband or partner of an AF you will find you have two careers. Your 'secondary' career is your normal 9-5 job for which you receive a salary.

Your 'primary' career, however, is being the partner to an AF. This will be a 24-hour, seven days a week, unpaid job, with few benefits, no holidays, and no prospects of promotion. Some may feel more comfortable calling it a vocation than a job and for many it certainly provides a purpose in life. But it will not be a cushy option, especially alongside your actual job.

Many AF husbands and partners find that life under two bosses is too hard and they resign from their 9-5 job in order to serve their AF more fully. Often the husband or partner's salary is not missed when it's gone and the man's self-esteem needs to be monitored after he gives up his day job.

Some of the perks of the job

You call but find you can't get a table at a good restaurant for yourself and a mate to have lunch. You know exactly what to do. You call back a few minutes later and try again under your wife's name. Miraculously, this time, you get the table.

This perk and many others like it can be derived from being associated with a woman of substance, an AF.

She's better known than you and she spends more than you, so she has better relationships with shops, airlines, restaurants and all manner of suppliers and merchants. They know her name and they take her seriously. And as her man you are fully permitted, indeed expected, to ride along in the wake of this advantage.

If she is an A grade AF she will have loyalty cards, credit cards, membership cards – VIP cards that give her access to every nook and cranny of luxury life. Chauffeur to the airport, no problem. Upgrade when you get there, no problem. Last minute table at The Wolseley, no problem. Tickets to the Premiere, box at the theatre, invitations to that celeb-infested party, no problem, no problem, no problem.

Before you met her you were hanging out with losers in the local pub. Now you are gently wafting past Colin Firth at the upstairs bar of Cut. Don't look too pleased with yourself but quietly celebrate it all.

Dealing with the social stigma

Being a man married to a woman with a higher social standing than you, with more money, a better job, classier friends and a genuinely unassailable superiority in every area, can lead to humiliation in certain social situations.

For example, when asked if you look after the kids while your wife brings home the bacon. Or when she is asked for business advice ahead of you. Or when asked what you do for a living and it is clearly far less important than what your AF does. Or whether she 'wears the trousers' etc.

Obviously humiliation is ghastly, needs to be avoided at all costs, and is a very real daily proposition if a strategy is not put in place to deal with it. There are four tried and tested strategies that work in most situations...

1. Light heartedly humiliate yourself before someone else does...

2. Don't ever go out socially. [This is clearly drastic but we do know one man who has chosen this route and although he will die a hermit, he is highly unlikely to ever be humiliated.]

3. Develop a long and baffling speech that purports to describe your work and exalted status, using complicated, technical terms.

4. Drink heavily at all social engagements, wear a scarf and pretend to be a mysterious, all-knowing Svengali who is the real power behind everything your AF has achieved.

Your mates will laugh

If you're married to an AF or living with an AF, your mates will think it's extremely funny. They will think you live under her thumb [you may well do]. They will think that you live in a permanent state of servility and even fear [ditto]. They will think you are a bit of a loser who plays second fiddle to his wife and who deserves to have the piss taken out of him at every opportunity.

But. When they are in the presence of your AF, those same mates will be just a little frightened. They will become all the things they mock you for. They will be in awe of her and will know that if they put one foot wrong she will be able to cut them to ribbons with a few choice remarks.

At the same time, a small part of them will nevertheless be drawn to her. Somewhere inside them will be the stirrings of attraction. You might call it the 'Margaret Thatcher Syndrome'. The men around her will be more than a little mesmerised by her and what she represents. They may not be able to think it through properly because they are men and their feelings will be always just beyond their full understanding, but they will feel something.

Under interrogation your mates might even voice these feelings of attraction, and they might come to realise why you are married to this woman ... that a life with her might be more than just material

for endless jokes, and that, given the chance, they

might even consider life with an AF themselves.

Don't compete with her gay friends – you'll lose

Every AF has a coterie of gay male friends. They perform a number of functions...

1. They worship her as a strong woman [and possibly a role model]

2. They dance

3. They compliment her on her clothes [and actually know the names of the designers who designed them]

4. They take her to events you can't be arsed to go to

5. They scream at her jokes

As a heterosexual male you will not be able to deliver on any of the above more than very occasionally. Plus, many of her single gay friends have 'Gay Energy'. They are not knackered from dealing with kids, mothers-in-law, domestic routine and the constant male versus female war of attrition that can wear a straight man's hair off. With this 'Gay Energy' her friends are always in the right frame of mind to deliver the fun that an AF needs. You are not.

Do not under any circumstances try to keep up. You will look like a fool if you mug up on women's fashion, ask her to go clubbing at Whisky Mist, compliment her every time she walks through the door, and scream when she makes a joke or does a funny dance move.

She will know what you are up to. She will hate you for trying to ingratiate yourself by 'Playing Gay'. No! Encourage her to have fun with her gay friends, safe in the knowledge that she is enjoying the company of other men but is extremely unlikely to end up shagging them.

Be the last to know

It is quite common to read about your AF in newspapers, magazines and websites, and to find out stuff that you didn't actually know, even though you've been together for years and have a 'No Secrets' policy in your relationship. [Example: One of the contributors to this book found out his AF was pregnant by reading the *Evening Standard*.]

Many AFs are newsworthy. The press love a high-achieving woman and a lot of journalists are fellow AFs who will delight in shedding light on one of their own.

Your only strategy as an AF husband or partner is to sign up to Twitter and Google Alerts and opt in for the latest news about your AF. That way you will be in the vanguard of people who get the freshest news from and about your woman and you will at least be as well informed as an ardent fan. This, for most purposes, is well informed enough.

Schmooze her PA

Your AF quite likely has a secretary or PA because she is busy and successful. You probably don't because you're probably not. Her PA books your AF's flights [and therefore yours]. Her PA runs her social life [and therefore yours]. Crucially, however, it's her PA that also decides how much access you get to your AF, so you'd better start schmoozing her.

Failing to get your AF's secretary on side could mean you will find yourself flying Economy, while your AF sits in Business or First ['Sorry, flight overbooked']. Or, you might find that you're not invited to key parties. [One contributor to this book tells a chilling story about falling out with his AF''s PA and not receiving an invitation to his own anniversary party.]

Most importantly, if you fail to schmooze the PA, you will find access to your AF mysteriously difficult, and you will start getting the same brush-off as her unwanted callers. ['She's in a meeting'... 'She's lunching with a client'... 'She's at the dentist'.]

Warning: It is a good tactic to be friendly towards the PA, to take a little time to talk to her and to remember her birthday. Do not, however, fall into the trap of being over-familiar and coming across as flirtatious. If your AF finds out, and if the PA is good, your AF will find it easier to get rid of you than her. So tread carefully.

How the Alpha Female negotiates

With her male boss – calmly and boldly

With her female boss – calmly and cautiously

With her girlfriends – fairly and normally

With you – she doesn't

Enjoy your own company

AFs are experts at filling their lives. They don't fill them with trivia, they fill them with important, meaningful, worthwhile stuff such as work, female relationships, self-improvement activities, acquisition, travel and culture.

You, on the other hand, have less to do. You may work and have a couple of mates but you simply can't think of other stuff to do in the same way as a motivated and directional AF. For example, you are happy on the sofa watching football for several hours a week, just the sort of inactivity your AF would be horrified by and regard as an unproductive waste of time.

These two different approaches to time management mean you will be spending a lot of time on your own ... get used to your own company.

Useful suggestions for filling your time...

- Talking to yourself
- Daydreaming
- Googling yourself and your mates
- Walking around naked
- Reading cereal packets

Over time you will learn to look to yourself for entertainment, support, pep talks, sympathy, advice and love.

Don't become the woman

After years of living with an AF, with her awesome superiority gently gnawing away at your manhood [and not in a nice way either], it is possible to get Gender Slippage [GS] ... where the male imperceptibly begins to slip into the role of the female.

When the husband or partner works shorter hours than his AF for example and he is on his own at home more often than he'd like, he may occasionally find himself filling the time with what is called IIH or 'Involuntary Instinctive Housekeeping'.

It may start innocently enough, with him rearranging the position of a vase, or putting clothes in the laundry basket. But it will quite often end with the male performing a whole set of full-on household tasks. These will include cooking slightly elaborate meals, noticing dust for the first time in his life, and cleaning it, loading the dishwasher and actually switching it on.

He may even start fussing over things that were never on his radar at all before, such as bathroom towels, curtains, bedspreads and, god forbid, even candles. In extreme cases, before too long he has become the woman in the relationship. This is the kiss of death.

No AF wants her man to become a woman. She doesn't want to come home to find him plumping the cushions and picking out braiding. She wants him to care, certainly, but she doesn't want him to be wearing the metaphorical pinny.

Warning: Gentlemen, if you suddenly catch yourself slowing down outside a drapery shop, or researching valences, give yourself a short, sharp pep talk and reclaim your masculinity in one or more of the following ways...

- Find a seedy bar and man up with two or three shots of Jack Daniels.

- Flirt with anyone of the opposite sex. Most of the time of course you will be ignored but occasionally you will get a sympathetic smile which will make you feel virile for the rest of the week.

- Take up wrestling.

- Make a show of raising your voice in a macho fashion when your AF is within earshot – on the phone, for example, to the speaking clock.

Basic rules for the Alpha Female's husband or partner

1. Never interrupt her
2. Never criticise her
3. Never be too tired for anything, especially sex
4. Don't ever be ill

She has inhabited my brain

After a while the partner of an AF will realise it is easier to let her do the thinking. His life will be smoother if he aligns his opinions more closely to hers.

You will know your brain has been totally aligned to hers when you are asked by someone else for your thoughts on a certain topic and you turn to your AF to ask... 'Darling, what do *I* think on that particular subject?'

Caveat: Sometimes this mind-melding can go too far. One contributor to this book relayed the terrifying story, that after seven years with his AF, he was no longer able to explain the offside rule, but knew the best places in London and New York to buy vintage Kelly bags.

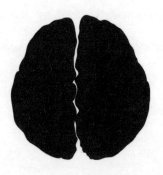

Sometimes it's about you

There are certain topics, solely relating to you, where your AF will always be prepared to give you the benefit of her help and advice, i.e...

- Your job and how you can do it better

- Your clothes and what's wrong with them

- Your body and what's wrong with it

- Your friends and what's wrong with them

- Your politics

- Your breath

- Your hair

Her To-Do List

This will be long and impossible for any man to fit into a single day. It will also be gloriously varied and will sometimes contain seemingly contradictory entries.

Examples... 'Breakfast at The Wolseley' followed by 'Start 5:2 Diet'.

Or... 'Practise 20 mins of Harmonious Mindfulness' followed by 'Fire the gardener'.

Pocket money

Known in the trade as 'Mousekeeping', pocket money is handed out by the AF to her man at times when he is earning little or indeed nothing. It is money that he does not have to 'work' for and so it is always welcome.

She doesn't see her partner as a charity case exactly but she feels he needs financial help every now and then, and she enjoys being the person to give it. She gives it out of love. She gives it to remind herself how well she has done in life. She also gives it as a sweet reminder of who's in charge!

Note: Mousekeeping must be accepted with gratitude certainly, but it must also be made clear to the AF that money is only money: Over-gratitude makes it too obvious to the AF that the man thinks there's no way on earth he could earn the money for himself, and that he is dependent on her. This is not a good look and can be disastrous for libido on both sides.

Alpha Female husbands and partners - your main 'Areas of Control' [AOC]

1. Garbage disposal

2. Changing light bulbs

3. Unblocking lavatories

4. Gas leaks

5. Long distance driving [valuable emailing time for her]

6. Heavy lifting

7. Anything else dangerous

Rare occasions when an Alpha Female stops being an Alpha Female

- Under general anaesthetic
- While watching *Downton Abbey*
- Upon the death of her pet
- Shortly after her own death
- When she bumps into an ex-boyfriend who is much hotter than you
- After crashing your car [but only for a few minutes]
- When she's being goofy and girly with her goofiest, girliest girlfriends

So you think you can argue

Trying to win an argument with an AF is like trying to out-box a young Muhammad Ali. Getting her own way and being right about things is an AF's natural state and her arguing skills are honed to this end.

Determination, courage, creativity, emotional intelligence, mental agility, and some underhand tricks men have never heard of, are a few of the tools that she will have at her disposal. She will have an alarming ability to recall facts, dates and names and a magical ability to convince you of something that clearly was never true.

She will sometimes surprise you by losing an argument but this is only because she WANTS to. Perhaps she is in a hurry to go out with her friends and does not want to waste valuable time. Or she is ovulating and requires sex urgently.

Desperate stratagems: You will never really win an argument with an AF but you could in extreme circumstances employ the following spoiler tactics...

1. walk away when she is in mid flow [dangerous]
2. agree with everything she says but in an obviously sarcastic way [equally dangerous]
3. laugh at everything she says [this is the equivalent of 'going nuclear' and will probably

result in the quick and terminal deterioration

of the relationship]

4. hum loudly with fingers in ears [sometimes

has same outcome as above]

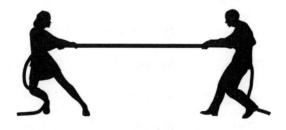

The man's opinion is highly valued. Then ignored

AFs will occasionally ask their partners for advice. This could be on a wide range of subjects, from curtains and wall colours, to business decisions, hair and fashion choices. Don't be fooled into thinking the relationship is a democracy, however. Your advice is asked for, listened to, but it will be ignored. When a man asks for advice he wants advice. When the AF asks for advice she is merely 'Thinking Out Loud'.

Example: Your AF is going out for the evening, either with you, or quite likely, without you. She wants to know that she is picking out the best outfit for the evening and is putting an enormous amount of mental effort and strategy into it.

She comes to you as her trusted male partner and asks you which dress she should wear, showing you two or three options. [As a man it is clear to you which dress is best – it's the one you fancy her in most – but to her it's a much deeper issue and there are many questions going on in her head.] She asks you which dress she should wear and as you are telling her your thoughts on the matter you notice 'the Glaze' – that far-off look in her eye that tells you she is not hearing a word you say and that her thoughts are miles away. Instead her brain is making the 4 million calculations per second necessary to produce an answer on the intensely complicated matter of outfit choice.

Console yourself with the knowledge that, although she hasn't listened to your 'advice', you have been a comfort to her. You have been there in a moment of real need. You have warmed the air nearby and you have helped her make her decision by allowing her to think out loud at a critical time.

Lose your loser friends

Now that you are with an AF, everything has moved up a gear. In your AF's orbit there is little room for chaos, misbehaviour or mental and physical untidiness. Everything and everybody needs a purpose, a direction and a raison d'etre. This includes you. It also includes your mates.

Male friends of yours that you considered fun, spontaneous and entertaining, will be seen by her in an altogether different light. If they do not deliver something special, socially or materially, these guys will be considered by your AF to be 'Losers'.

She will be too clever to come right out and describe them as 'Losers' to your face, but you will notice over time that she has gently, bit by bit, edited them out of your life.

In 'AF World', picking people to adorn your life together is done with the same exquisite care as picking out furnishings, wall coverings and art. And with much the same end in sight. They need to be a credit to your AF, adding a little extra lustre, value and status to her social life. Friends are not there for your entertainment, this is a male concept and not understood by the AF.

After one or two years with your AF, take a look around and you will notice that your unsavoury old chums have been replaced by a new crowd of metrosexual achievers, mini celebs, hard-working movers and shakers and useful contacts. Mentally put your old friends in a drawer like you did with your childhood teddy bear and enjoy your glittering new social life.

Your clothes [and how they affect her image]

Your AF's clothes and the way she dresses are her business and her business alone and your input into the way she looks is one of the classic 'Relationship Minefields'. Offering advice, even when asked, must be done with extreme caution.

Your clothes and the way you dress are also her business and are, at all times, up for discussion, comment and 'constructive criticism'.

The AF normally likes to see her man well turned out at all times. This creates an image that makes you [by which we mean her] look good. In a suit for example her man looks: a] employed, b] tidy, c] sane, d] grown up.

And even if none of these things are true, indeed especially if none of them are true, the suit will fool most people for long enough.

Remember, the clothes you wear must always be appropriate and never make her look bad.

Partnered to an AF, expect a lifetime's advice on the way you look. Accept it with good grace [often she'll be correct]. Repeat the oft quoted mantra 'happy wife, happy life', say goodbye lightly to autonomy in the wardrobe department.

The Marks-Partridge Alpha Scale

It's important to know how to rate an AF. Whether it's for business purposes, in social situations, or because you're dating, married, or about to become involved with one, knowing the extent of a woman's 'Alpha-ness' and where she sits on the MPAS is vital information.

Alpha Minus

The most man-friendly type, and in fact, only mildly Alpha. You can expect to get your way as much as 20% of the time [this sounds like heaven to those men living with AFs further up the Marks-Partridge Scale] and indeed even to dominate in certain areas. Remember, however, she is still an AF and will sometimes display AF characteristics.

Would suit: A thinking man who likes a quiet life with only occasional flashes of intense stress.

Alpha Standard

She knows she's an AF. She revels in most or all of the behaviours outlined in this book. She is strong and independent and capable of living without you [or any man] completely. As her partner you can expect to have 11.5% control of your life at best and 0.00012% control at worst. If you ever find yourself getting your own way, it is because of a momentary oversight on her part.

Would suit: A phlegmatic man who used to be successful but has taken his foot right off the gas.

Alpha Plus

Should be approached with caution. You are now deep in Alpha territory.

The Alpha Plus is easily recognised. She dominates boardrooms, eats rival CEOs for breakfast, keeps a perfect home and physique, and still finds time to remind you to record *Downton Abbey* for her on a

Sunday night. As her partner you are on full alert at all times. You can, however, relax a little if she's abroad. [The rule of five applies here – you can relax a little more if she's away for more than five days and is further than 5000 miles away.]

Note: Subduing a fired-up Alpha Plus should never be attempted without a tried and tested escape route.

Would suit: A good-looking man with scant achievements who needs somebody else to 'drive the bus'.

<u>Alpha Plus Plus</u>

Probably to be avoided unless you are a masochist or you have bone where your brain should be. This woman sleeps standing up, crunches diamonds between her teeth and makes Boudicca and Angela Merkel look like a pair of pussies. In other words, DEFCON 1 IN A PAIR OF HEELS.

Would suit: A man in a long-term vegetative state who can feel no pain.

Her kit is better than yours

Leaving the house at the same time as your AF can be a painful reminder that her kit is better than yours. You bite your lip as you see her roar off in her BMW, Audi or, God forbid, Porsche. As you climb into your knackered old banger or the family estate car, you pretend it doesn't matter, but it does.

Flash cars, once a male preserve, are now wide open to the successful AF. You may know better than her what goes on under the bonnet [actually you don't] but it's academic because cars don't break down any more and anyone can buy one and use it without having to know the difference between a spark plug and a brake disc.

Unthinkable 30 years ago, there are now cars specifically MADE for women, targeted at women, designed for women ... really good, expensive, desirable cars. The same thing applies to many other toys and gadgets. Because your woman is an AF she knows how to use them all and she wants to own them all.

Her phone will be the best on the market, as will her laptop. Her tablet will be better than yours [you may not even have one]. In fact, everything she owns will be better and newer than everything you own.

There are three ways to realistically deal with this problem...

1. you go 'Eco' or 'Hipster'. In other words, you pretend that you prefer old technology because you are renouncing meaningless consumerism.

2. you get her to buy you some better stuff at Christmas.

3. you use her stuff when she's not looking.

You thought you had good taste. You don't

In the same way that your AF will subtly remove all your 'Loser' mates from the equation, she will also gradually remove all the 'Stuff' that you have bought and treasured over the years. Stuff that represented your experiences, your history, your passions and your unique taste.

As the man of the house and as the AF's dearly beloved, you will be allowed to keep one or two prized objects about the house. A painting, a chair, a photograph; but these objects will need to be chosen by your AF, not by you. Also, bear in mind, even these precious pieces may too disappear over time, normally during a re-organisation or a refurbishment. Or when you are away, for example, on a stag weekend.

In extreme cases, items of yours that go missing may get sold on eBay or 'down-cycled' [thrown away]. However, most of the time the AF will merely put them in storage, to be given back to you in the event of a terminal bust-up, or to be disposed of once you have entirely forgotten about their existence.

Fortunately for the AF very few men will fight to the death to hold on to items that have been chosen by him to adorn the home. Most men will give up quite quickly when their furnishings or decorative items are under threat and may in some cases even feel a little relieved to let the AF take over. Somewhere lurking inside most men there is a self-doubt around aesthetic judgment, particularly as far as home decor is concerned, and this self-doubt, being a weakness, is successfully exploited by the seldom self-doubting AF.

Like many battles between the AF and her man, this one is not worth fighting, she will win anyway, and the collateral damage will be you.

**Things she can say to you but you can't say back
to her**

- Do you really want that extra dessert?

- You're drinking too much.

- Make yourself useful.

- It's time to go home.

- We're spending the holidays with my family
  this year.

- I've got a headache.

- No.

Tactical honesty

Bearing in mind your main reason for living is to make her happy, sometimes a little dishonesty and telling her what she wants to hear, will go a long way. Things you may need to lie about...

1. Which of her friends you fancy

2. Which of her friends you hate

3. That outfit she loves that you never liked

4. Her snoring

Decision-Making

One of the many dangers for husbands and partners of Alpha Females is losing any powers of decision-making you were once endowed with.

Since every decision you make is checked [and frequently overturned] by her, the part of the brain that used to be engaged in independent decision-making can atrophy from underuse.

Keep your brain in training with some simple daily decision-making tasks. For example:

- Cornflakes or Weetabix in the morning?
- Sit or stand to pee?
- Vodka or lager when out with your mates?

One of the authors of this book recounts a chilling tale of a man's DMC [Decision Making Cortex] that had become so withered that he could no longer decide between boxers and Y-fronts, and so wore both...

Six things the Alpha Female won't do

1. Be the first to apologise or make up

2. 'Nurse'

3. Walk to you when she can shout

4. Anything vague or unplanned

5. Leave a party early because you're tired or not feeling well

6. Stay at a party late if she's tired or not feeling well

Exes

Get used to seeing, discussing and involving your Alpha Female's ex-boyfriends. They are an integral part of her life, and therefore your life.

Get used also to not seeing, discussing and involving your ex-girlfriends. You will probably find that they have been ex-communicated, redacted and de-registered from history by your AF. Although her exes will be welcome in her [and therefore your] life, your exes will be about as welcome as a clutch of flatulent skunks.

Tools available to the Alpha Female's husband or partner in times of crisis

- The whispered remark [just out of earshot]

- Crying [should be used very sparingly and tactically]

- An affair [for the word 'affair' read 'suicide']

- Your therapist

- Drugs and alcohol

Tools never available to the Alpha Female's husband or partner

- Relying on any ancient notion of male superiority.

Three's a crowd

There are three people in this relationship. You, your Alpha Female and her smartphone. Most of the space you would have occupied, and want to occupy, before its invention, is now taken by it.

It's the first thing she touches in the morning, and the last thing to soothe her to sleep at night. It's constantly in her pocket or her hand, or pressed lovingly to her cheek. It's her connection to the world and it whispers sweet nothings in her ear.

Suggestion: stay calm, recognise how important her phone is to her and go with it. You may even wish to carry a spare charger with you. In this way you can ensure that you will not end up being the brunt of a potentially dangerous mood-swing brought on by a flat battery.

Second fiddle

Because your AF is more important than you, in social situations, get used to people asking how she is before asking how you are.

It will sting a little each time you get ignored, barged out of the way or trampled on by people who are more interested in her than they are in you. This is never going to be easy to deal with, but it is something you are going to have to learn to swallow.

There will be many other ways in which you will be reminded of your SFS [Second Fiddle Status].

You will be placed at the riff-raff end of the table at dinner parties; she will be next to the host. All successes in your life will be somehow attributed to her and all failures will be attributed to you.

Not only her family, but your family too, will address all matters of importance to her rather than to you. Decisions that you thought you had made, she will overturn, and of course her agenda will always triumph over yours, in every area.

Our advice to you as a man in this position is to breathe deeply and let go. Let go of your ego. Let go of your agenda and replace it with hers. Surrender with a smile. Develop a Zen-like calm and let her drive.

How your Alpha Female sees you

An AF husband or partner will fall into one of the following four categories. Clearly the final two are dangerous categories to be in and may spell the end of the relationship. An AF husband or partner can, with skill and effort, move into a better category if it is not too late. The categories are...

1. Rock star [you overhear her compare you to a famous musician or actor who she fancies. Although she is the only person who can see the resemblance]

2. Pet [you overhear her say she feels 'comfortable and safe' with you]

3. Rock [see next chapter]

4. Invisible man [uh oh]

Man as rock

If you ever hear your AF telling someone you are 'her Rock' you may be in trouble.

What she actually means [and she may not even know this herself] is that she sees you as dependable and solid, but alas, also predictable and boring. She knows you are always going to be around, she sees you as part of the furniture, and she is possibly starting to take you for granted.

No woman wants to shag a rock and no man wants to be described as one – wet and cold, grey and heavy. A rock star certainly, but never a rock.

Alarm bells will sound to the sensible man, on first hearing himself being described as a rock. He will realise he has just heard his AF issue her first verbal warning. He will be alert enough to calculate that he needs to make changes and inject a little more excitement before his relationship begins to slide.

[See later chapter on 'freshening your relationship']

Your genes

At a certain point in a man's life [normally about the age of 38] a little tiny messenger starts to run backwards and forwards between his head and his testicles, opening a previously non-existent dialogue. It will range across a number of very important subjects, none of which will have been properly debated before. Subjects such as 'Life', 'Death', 'Relationships' and 'Children'.

[It will be astonishing to a woman that this debate starts so bewilderingly late in a man, but up until that point in his life he has been busy with another all engaging subject... 'Himself'.]

The testicles have a role in this debate because the underlying, unspoken driver of the discussion is the man's genes. And sex, rather than being only for fun, can also be used as a method for making little versions of himself.

Eventually, and it might take a few years, the man will somehow work out for himself that the better the woman he breeds with, the better protected his genes will be.

Once this realisation has been achieved, the man will instinctively know that the Gorgeous But Stalky Chick, the Hot But Vacant Chick, the Busty But Neurotic Chick are not the best women for the job ... although they had always been his favourite types up to this point.

Indeed, the best enabler for his genes and their journey into the future is the switched-on, organised, motivated, reliable, interesting, strong, independent, entertaining, successful, dynamic, Grade A woman. The Alpha Female.

Slight Caveat: The Extreme AF has genes so strong that in many cases they may obliterate the genes of the male completely and their offspring will look like her rather than him.

Sex. Your moment to be in charge [or not]

Early in your life with an AF you will become aware of the reversal of your relationship's power dynamic that takes place in the bedroom. Whilst your Alpha Female may dominate every other sphere of her life [and yours], in bed you are expected to take charge.

The Alpha Female likes sex and her body courses with all the right powerful hormones. Her fast and furious lifestyle raises her libido, and as her partner you will need to be ready for the call to action at any time.

At short notice you will be expected to transform from being a supportive, attentive, empathetic Beta Male outside the bedroom, into a raging, dominating, hard-shagging Alpha bastard inside it. Sex is the one and only arena where this sort of behaviour is encouraged, indeed expected. Your AF will not appreciate you being weak, indecisive or submissive in the 'chambre de bataille' and your relationship will descend into farce very quickly if you are.

Important:

- Sex could be your area to shine. In fact, get this right and many good things will follow. It may even paper over some of the cracks in other areas of the relationship.

- Denying your AF sex is one of the few, if not the only, real powers you will ever possess. But be warned, use it sparingly.

- On a happier note, one good shag has been known to make certain AFs drop their 'Alphaness' for up to 2.5 hours.

Important Final Point: All of the above should be taken with a pinch of salt because, at all times, whilst appearing to be in control and doing what YOU want in bed, you both know you're only really there to deliver what SHE wants.

The Alpha Female hierarchy of loves and needs

- Her work

- Her parents and siblings

- Her friends

- Her PA

- Her smartphone

- Her pet[s]

- Her home[s]

- Her bags

- Her shoes

- Her cleaner

- You

Who pays?

In a restaurant, at the end of a meal when the waiter arrives with the bill, as the husband of an AF, it's important you know what to do next.

In a practised way, you nod the bill subtly over in her direction. She knows what's going on because she isn't stupid and she colludes because she doesn't want to humiliate you in public [this time]. She pays the bill.

When you are married to or living with an AF, the money dynamic is different to that in a male-dominated relationship. The AF has her own money and often she will have more than her man, so there will be instances when she will be paying for things.

In a way, this works badly for both parties. The man feels humiliated and loser-ish. The woman feels used and too dominant. But it is essential that both parties find a way to make it work and for most couples this will only happen over time as a secret, silent language is developed to make the act of paying invisible to outsiders.

Useful tips:

- The internet is a good place to shop and use the AF's credit card in private.
- Taking a bundle of cash out of the ATM on her card will enable you to carry funds and look like the man you want to be.

Marital arts

Extremely rarely, and if sufficiently provoked by you, your AF may give you a series of looks that are so murderous that you fear for your wellbeing. These looks can cause something akin to real pain in the less habituated male. Here are the rules for defending yourself against such looks...

1. Try to parry her murderous glances by covering your face with a cushion [not one of her valuable vintage silk ones]

2. Bob and weave until her eyeballs tire of following you around the room

3. Run away whilst apologising loudly

4. Drop to the floor and play dead

The TV remote

A small point but one worth mentioning: Occasionally you will be allowed to hold and operate the TV remote while you watch TV together.

However, your AF is only allowing this to happen because it is more convenient for her to tell you when to change channel than it is to do it herself.

In short, if you are holding the remote, you are the remote.

Conversation stealer

Do not be alarmed if you notice your AF stealing some of your conversations, ideas and witticisms. It may even be a form of flattery.

Obviously most of the stuff that comes out of your brain and your mouth will be football and movie-trivia related nonsense, but every now and then you will accidentally come up with a good insight or conversation piece. [One of the authors of this book for example has a theory that the overflow holes in baths are not big enough because he still manages to flood the bathroom on a regular basis.]

Having aired such conversational nuggets, and if they have gone down well, you may then find them hijacked or borrowed at strategic points by your AF.

The better they are received by the audience, the less likely you are to get credited for them. Look on the bright side, however, if a theory or anecdote of yours goes down like a shit sandwich when told by your AF, you will be credited immediately.

Freshening your relationship

This of course is your job not hers. If some corner [or indeed all] of your relationship has gone stale, the unspoken rule is that it is your fault. You are the one who should have taken the initiative to set up date-nights, mini-breaks, romantic interludes, and 'spontaneous' moments. She, after all, is too busy.

If the dreaded day arrives when she tells you that some of the 'spark' has gone out of your relationship, what she is really saying is 'I'm bored and it's your fault'. So the authors of this book have come up with a few tried and tested tips for putting the life back into your relationship. Bear in mind, your woman is an AF with very high standards so no ordinary stuff will do...

- A Faux Bohemian Weekend. Your AF will like to think she is a simple creature and a relaxed hippy at heart [she is neither of course but it is a good look]. So set up a weekend at a rustic 7-star hotel where the food is locally sourced and the ambience includes wood-burning stoves and views. She will be reinvigorated by the simple pleasures of Ruinart champagne and artisan olives, lying on cashmere throws and looking at the stars through the triple glazed skylight above the hotel bed, and of walks from the hotel bedroom to the hotel spa.

- A Cultural Experience. Try a visit to an Ai Weiwei exhibition, for example, or to the theatre. It will do wonders for her and therefore also for you. Note: Avoid anything that will get her too fired up, however, about geo-political issues. This could become fuel for an argument between you in the cab home afterwards and take the shine off the whole endeavour.

- Or anything else that will look good on her social media feeds. A series of impressive Instagrams posted by your AF from an exclusive happening or an eye-watering location will spread good feeling amongst her social group and this can only reflect well on all concerned.

Flattery

The AF's one true weak spot is flattery. With everything else she has a gimlet eye for insincerity, manipulation or subterfuge, but when it comes to flattery she is blind and powerless.

Gentlemen, if you take nothing else from this book, remember this one lesson, flattery is the Kryptonite of the AF. With it you have the ability to reduce her powers [temporarily] such that she becomes putty in your hands.

- You have a free hand here to use the approach you think will work best. You know your AF better than anyone but remember always to flatter her brain as well as her looks ... e.g. 'My darling, I really need your advice/opinion/input on something very important. You have a way, unlike anybody else I know, of scything through and getting to the very heart of something. Having access to your planet-sized brain surely makes me the luckiest man on earth.' Look deeply into her eyes at this point and if possible summon up a little tear.

She'll probably need a wife [or wives] of her own

Your AF works hard and plays hard. Every minute of her day is productive and although she is eminently capable of performing all the homemaking duties herself she will have more important things to do.

You, as a well-trained husband or partner, will pitch in as best you can, but you are a man so your attention to detail around the house will fall short of what your woman requires. She is therefore left with no option but to find herself a 'wife'.

We have to be careful here because we are tiptoeing across a feminist firing range, but let's just say that a woman is often best at delivering what another woman wants when it comes to running a home. For a start she will have the vocabulary. She will know what a 'topper' is, what 'curling tongs' are for, what an 'emery board' is. She will also know why things have to be cleaned even when they are out of sight. Which flowers to buy and how to display them. When supplies of kitchen towel and couscous are running low. And a million other things.

These are all things that no man will ever master, however metrosexual he tries to become. So a female housekeeper or cleaner, au pair or nanny [or all of the aforementioned] will be needed to step in.

Finding such a woman is notoriously hard.

She will have to go through a set of soul-baring interviews with your AF, followed by a trial period. She will have to have a broad skill set ranging from cleaning all the way through to cooking, household management and childcare. She will have to be presentable [obviously not 'hot' which would be distracting for you], calm, intelligent, diligent and subservient and sensitive enough to the AF so as not to step on her toes or threaten her territory.

Once this 'wife' [or 'wives' plural] has been found, your life and that of your AF will improve immeasurably. Only a foolish man will fail to see the benefits of his wife having a wife of her own, and to my knowledge there has never been a single case of an AF's husband or partner trying to prevent it from happening.

Expanded vocabulary

New words and terms for you to memorise. You never knew they existed when you were a single man but now, as the husband or partner of an AF, you will need to be ready to hear them, understand them, and use them to great effect whenever required...

- Kale

- Celine

- Wellness

- Manolo Blahnik

- Nutribullet

- 5:2

- Yogalates

- Sorry

Weapons in the Alpha Female arsenal

- The freezeout [pretending you don't exist]

- Cockmail [withholding sex]

- Cashmail [withholding money]

When she's away

Of course, once you are committed to an AF in a long-term relationship, the word 'freedom' may represent a cruel mirage.

Your AF exerts control in every area of your life, and you have long since succumbed to a kind of Stockholm Syndrome, where you identify strongly with the needs and desires of the other person and profoundly confuse your own wishes and requirements with hers.

This makes it disorientating when your AF suddenly goes away for a period of time, on a business trip perhaps or a holiday with girlfriends, and the potential for a small parcel of actual freedom presents itself to you.

If you are lucky, friends will rally round and keep you on the rails at such a critical time. Not unlike a 'lifer' who has just been released from prison, you are vulnerable when presented with the heady choices that newfound freedom present. You are susceptible to the following:

- Confusion
- Overexcitement
- Rashes
- Bingeing [on drugs, food, booze, fun]
- Thinking you are attractive to other women

You will also instantly re-establish all the habits that your AF has discouraged you from enjoying – things such as nose-picking, public ball-scratching, eating high-fat processed food for every meal, drinking beer in the mornings, whistling, spending an hour on the loo, listening to very loud rap music with middle-aged mates, peppering your conversation with words like 'ragga' and 'ballin', and not shaving or washing.

And finally you will dig out the clothes that your AF will not allow you to wear when she is around. The hip-hop inspired trainers and the too-baggy or too-skinny trousers will come out, the old T-shirt collection, the baseball hat possibly, and indeed any item of clothing that relates to your 'Heyday' [which only exists in your mind].

But remember, there's no hiding place

Husbands and partners of an AF always bear in mind, her powers of awareness and control over others are considerable.

In a way that may seem superhuman to you, her man, your AF will always be able to keep tabs on you, wherever you are, at home or abroad, night and day. She will always know your whereabouts.

This is partly a female thing anyway. Every woman has a sixth sense about the location and activities of her loved ones at all times, but with the AF those powers are terrifyingly acute.

The AF knows all about communications technology so she will be able to find you via email, phone, Twitter, Facebook, fax, snail mail or satellite phone. And if that doesn't work she will send her PA to find you. And if that doesn't work she will have a network of friends [spies] all over the known world who will feedback relevant information to her on a regular basis.

In other words, wherever you are and whatever you're doing, if you are partnered to an AF, your movements and activities will be known to her. You belong to her so this is only fair. Get used to this lack of privacy and not having your own secret little corners in life because there ain't nothing you can do about it.

NB: One of the authors of this book recounts a chilling tale of mildly flirting with a woman he just met in a bar three thousand miles from home, only for the woman to take a call from his AF while they were talking.

The price of redemption

Errors or fuck-ups by you can be atoned for, by the appropriate act of redemption. The greater the fuck-up the bigger the act of redemption required. Here are some examples...

- Small argument when you're in the right – a small bunch of flowers and an apology
- Small argument when she's in the right – a big bunch of flowers and an apology
- Mistreating her dog – a sincere apology to the dog and dinner [for her, not the dog]
- Getting drunk and throwing up at her office party – a holiday in the Maldives

- Not recording *Downton Abbey* while she's away – two boxsets, flowers and an apology

- Getting caught watching porn – apologising to her parents and tea for them and her at Fortnum's

- Flirting with one of her mates – a weekend in Ibiza [without you]

- Forgetting her [your] wedding anniversary – a shopping trip to NY [this only works if she uses your money, not hers]

- Giving the wrong answer when asked how an outfit looks – a new pair of shoes

- Not noticing she's been to the hairdresser – chocolates

- Being ill – an apology plus jewellery

Types of sex with an Alpha Female

With the AF there's no such thing as just a shag. Each shag has an entirely different meaning and strategy behind it, and has to achieve a very specific goal. Here are a few examples...

The Spontaneous Shag

Carefully planned in every detail in advance by the AF to make her appear carefree, impulsive and sexy.

The Maintenance Shag

When your AF notices she has been ignoring you and possibly even mistreating you for some time.

She schedules in a cursory five minutes between other things and allows you to 'let off steam'.

The Anger Shag

This time SHE needs to let off steam after someone has said something horrible to her at work or one of her girlfriends has hinted that she is getting fat or old. She needs a fairly rough shagging and what she is really doing is using you as a kind of human punchbag or, more accurately, shagbag.

The Lazy Shag

This is a popular one with the men who live with an AF. She wants a shag because she is feeling relaxed and good about herself, but she can't be bothered to put in any effort at all. This is much like a normal shag in that respect, but the crucial difference here is that she is relaxed enough not to care if you are lazy about it too. A Lazy Fuck well executed will lead to the Holy Grail of Shags, maximum satisfaction with minimum effort.

The Accidental Bonus Shag

This happy occasion arrives once every now and then, unheralded and unexpected. It will always be the result of something highly agreeable happening to your AF, like a new pair of shoes or a promotion, that has heated her up so much that she gets the horn. If you are close by, you may be the lucky recipient of a Bonus Shag.

The Fuck-Fight

This is self-explanatory to anyone who has been in a long-term relationship. You can't have an actual fist fight with your AF obviously because you are a civilised, modern male but you can have a fuck-fight. If both parties are in the mood and have been a bit testy with each other for a while, a bit of appropriate and consensual rufty-tufty-rumpy-pumpy can go down well with both parties.

The Make-Up Fuck

This is not what you think. This is when you are shagging but your AF has only recently applied make-up ... so no kissing and no touching her face.

The Miserable Ending

We have all heard of the 'Happy Ending' offered by dodgy masseurs the world over. The 'Miserable Ending' is the antithesis of that. It occurs quite simply when, towards the end of a shag, just as you are about to 'shout bingo', your AF suddenly remembers:

a] that she has forgotten to email her girlfriend,

b] that she needs to make a call,

c] she should be somewhere else, or

d] she doesn't like you at the moment.

At such a point your AF exits stage left and leaves your littlest limb in limbo. This is not nice and can lead to an extremely unpleasant condition called blueballs if something is not done about it [by you] fairly swiftly.

The Procreation Shag

Get down the gym, get some nice loose underwear, start reading baby books, because she wants a baby! And when she does you'd better be up to it. No slacking, no headaches, no excuses, you're going to be shagging when her ovaries tell you to and you ain't going to be allowed to let up until you hear the pitter-patter of tiny feet.

She will die for you

It can be easy to forget, after a lifetime of training at the hands of your AF, that you are not just a set of functions, there to make your AF's life run more smoothly. It is easy to forget that, in her way, she loves you and needs you.

Don't be fooled by her powerful and capable demeanour. Don't make the mistake of thinking that you are not integral, that she can operate just as well [or better] without you.

She looks self-contained, self-confident and self-supporting, but, and this is very difficult to believe ... she depends on you. It is not just what you do for her in practical terms, you are the dumbbell that flexes her love muscles. You play an essential role in completing her, she needs you as a person, and as her man.

Once you have understood this, you will also come to realise that, actually, if ever the chips are down, she would die for you. She is the greatest ally you will ever have, and if necessary, she will throw all her power, her intellect and energy into helping you if you ever really need it.

Caveat: As heart-warming as it sounds, let's not get carried away. You are highly unlikely to require her to die for you, or even to take a small-gauge bullet in the leg for you, and, as a man, you will probably die well before her anyway.

In summary

After years of living with AFs [in what amounts to millions of hours of training and research] the authors of this book have been able to boil down what we have discovered into a few key learnings. If a man wants to survive, and even possibly thrive in a relationship with an Alpha Female he will need to be...

- Strong and assertive yet at the same time sensitive and malleable.

- Clean and well organised yet at the same time rugged and spontaneous.

- Hard working and busy but always available.

- Funny and sexy but not with other women.

- Practical but not boring.

- Opinionated as long as his opinions match his AF's.

- Masculine yet good with pets and shopping.

- Relaxed yet energetic.

- Soulful yet grounded.

- Exciting yet dependable.

- Generous [with your AF] yet frugal [with yourself].

- Understanding [with her family] yet ruthless [with your own].

- Confident yet humble.

- Romantic yet tough.

- A good nurse but never a patient.

- An animal in bed but a saint in all the other rooms of the house.

- Fit and strong but without spending hours exercising.

- A great cook and an even better washer-up.

- Mature yet young at heart.

- Endlessly supportive but never demanding.

- Well turned out but never vain.

- Yourself at all times ... yet the man she wants you to be at all times too.

Easy peasy. Good luck...